the complete absence of twilight

Howie Good

MadHat Press
Asheville, North Carolina

MadHat Press
MadHat Incorporated
PO Box 8364, Asheville, NC 28814

ISBN 978-1-941196-00-7 (paperback)

Cover art by Marc Vincenz
Book and cover design by MadHat Press

www.madhat-press.com

CONTENTS

quartet

1

I had just turned six. The universal symbol for handicapped hadn't been invented yet. Birds dragging broken wings left their black footprints on the stairs.

2

My parents made me take piano lessons. The piano hated me. I spent Hanukkah watching Christmas lights blink on and off on the house across the street.

3

My shadow walked ahead. It seemed odd that the stairs that went up were the same stairs that went down.

4

A man stood washing an apple at the sink. All the windows facing the other side of the world were open. Veiled women beckoned him into the Kasbah. The X on the sidewalk marks the spot where he landed.

dark city

1

I reached port by dusk, like a solution that somehow precedes discovery of the problem. A voice warned against betting on which sugar cube the fly would land on. Just then a man walked in and slammed a severed head down on the bar. "Give this bitch a drink," he said. That ended our night, but there was always tomorrow, with its iron bed and torn shade and ghost child playing on daddy's knee.

2

The ancients, when they traveled through forests, carried a cage of fireflies for light. A room is also just a kind of box. While I sleep, someone named Manfred Dada sends me a business proposition in an e-mail, and purple nights weather my skin silver-gray. It's impossible to tell from TV whether darkness is encroaching on the city or the city on darkness. A one-armed man plays the piano with both hands.

3

Despite the coat of dust on everything, winter retained some of its glitter. I waited half the morning at a crosswalk for the procession of weary shadows to pass. A building had collapsed as if overcome by grief. Survivors pointed to the numbers tattooed on their arms. More than a few could tell you the difference between a casket and a coffin. But it was the sincerity of the thunder and lightning that most impressed me. There wasn't much work available even for a person with a college degree.

4

Suits show up at my door one evening. They questioned the famous fictional characters that now live anonymously in the one-bedroom apartment in my head. I try to appear unconcerned. In a democracy, the women are free to pee standing up, the men sitting down.

5

A graveyard angel rides a Greyhound into town. Darkness is just as much a real color as red or white or blue. Drunk college students crowd the sidewalk and then vanish again when the killings resume. I warm my hands over a trash can fire, staring up in consternation at the grim parables lavishly retold in stained glass.

6

I hide behind a bush. The last free Indians on the Plains graze in the tall grass. One of them, when I look closer, is munching on insects. I uncurl my finger from the trigger. The dying light renders my face conveniently indistinct. Everyone has a lucky number, though some don't know what theirs is.

rsvp

I looked for the house while also trying to watch the road. The slower I drove, the harder it became. Up since sunrise, the bride was still combing her thinning brown hair. A guest had left a dead bird on the porch as a gift, curiously without any blood or marks of violence on it – nothing, the groom thought, a war can't fix. Everyone felt exiled from everyone else, but the minister after a few drinks greeted each of us familiarly. He seemed surprised that this was all my arms could hold.

blind man's bluff

There are so many cute little blondes that sometimes I confuse their names. Caffeine withdrawal intensifies the effect. Only later was the true source of the buzzing I heard revealed. And I had thought it was a winged horse trapped behind the glass! It's the kind of thing I like to ponder as I walk down to the corner mailbox, passing trees and windows and a dog chewing on a police whistle. I hardly even care if the mailbox isn't there, or if it is, that I can't see it.

and so on

Mr. Death visited a hospital out of professional curiosity, searched unsuccessfully for Yeats' grave throughout the south of France, walked on the beach in winter, when the ocean is flat and gray, the way he likes it. His interest now was in precise things – caliber, killing range, etc. – and as he considered whether to use a .22 on you or something poisonous, his face assumed the benign expression of a secret bomb factory.

marco polo

I sat in a room of eager doctoral students who nodded sagely even as the professor drew pentagrams on the board. Women with scratch 'n' sniff skin would enter my thoughts, but avoid leaving their names. The moon appeared from somewhere behind me like the holed white hull of a dream. There's a suspicion that Marco Polo did not tell half of what he saw. Birds of certain countries could sing in three languages and lie and grieve in none.

suspicion

Plainclothesmen prowled the train station all night. Everyone arriving on the 8:10 looked like a fugitive. An old junky who made his living stealing overcoats was followed by a parade of children chanting his name. The cops must have been waiting for someone else. In those days, a suspect sat on a stool with a hot spotlight on him, and no matter how much I begged, my parents wouldn't let me keep the motherless babies, slimy and blind, born in a dark corner of the garden.

waking up in recovery

It was late at night inside me. The nurse on duty believed in the therapeutic properties of art. Bullet-riddled bodies stood around my bed making small talk. Ethics was discussed back then, when it was discussed at all, as what you shouldn't do rather than what you should. No one I met considered it hypocrisy to dream in fragments, but bleed in full sentences.

remember the alamo

The God of Carnage
rides around in a shopping cart
& waves his stump on TV,
while a woman, living quietly,
picks ashes from her hair.

post-coital blues

I blew apart inside her,
fragments like super-bright truck headlights,
the shudder of a chair collapsing
under God's immense weight,
but the jackals that came afterwards
had grievances & no known address.

Howie Good

history is made at night

While
we somehow
sleep,

the old men
in orange
safety vests

scoop up
roadkill
with shovels

& fling it
into the future.

storm coming

1
I let the dog in.
Dogs don't leave
fingerprints.

2
Every sad utterance
of the wind is a lie.
Every word it writes down
has another spelling.

3
Fireworks are illegal,
the dark & sparkling memory
of a garbled dream.
All night I hold
a match to the fuse.

anniversary of a death

1

Freelance pallbearers hold a festival of growing things, Aurora glory Alice. Excessive heat, a long list of desserts, anti-psychotics – the minimum requirements.

2

Only me on the beach and empty mini-bottles of rum, the morning all to myself, a double yellow halo of sun smoke wrapped around my forehead pirate-fashion.

3

As sometimes happens, atoms exult. I am not the typical jackknifed tractor trailer nor a fishing boat, green with white trim, on waves of gray, late-blooming blue.

4

Eat sushi like you were going to rob a bank, ill-concealed though you are by a vase of table flowers.

magnetic disturbance

1

Summer has been halted at the border before. You can find carcasses if you look in the roadside ditches.

2

A woman appeared in the doorway clutching something pale and shriveled. *This,* she said, *is my mother's recipe.*

3

The dim pulse of the clock traveled up through the roots – one theory why there were no trees, only a broken white line down the center and a moonlighting cop shot in the head.

4

Flashlights beamed through the window whenever I tried to fall back asleep. A voice like a crow's leaked in under the door: *We must carry our grief alone.*

living in the spin cycle

It isn't actually a wrecked stock car. I just call it that, the top two floors occupied, and the lower 48 on fire. The mirror on the wall has mastered the technique of waiting graciously for someone to appear. Meanwhile, I listen to the insect-like buzz of my own blood in embarrassed silence. The only instruction is FOLLOW ALL INSTRUCTIONS. There are naked women everywhere. I don't think I'll be doing laundry.

politics as usual

1

Looters fled through your dreams with armfuls of gewgaws and groceries. Someone born without hands grew one. You pulled a small alarm clock set to Mountain Time out of your pocket. It hummed like a faint blue quasar.

2

You allowed only friends, and not of all of them, to call you Dick. Everyone else bowed their heads to read the headlines. Who couldn't use a drink first thing after waking up? Preposterously tall, you held onto the kitchen counter when the tree in the window shook.

3

The severed head you discovered lying on the carpet spoke a language you hadn't bothered to learn. His face was familiar, but his name eluded you. You may have noticed the sun slobbering all over the windows. Then it was time again for sleep.

the complete absence of twilight

When the clock you had shot couldn't be repaired, you placed it on a hill as bear bait. The floor of the forest was littered by then with the red-and-black checkered caps of hundreds of hunters. There was, your last postcard said, a complete absence of twilight. You should have lived to fifty or even fifty-five, a pint tucked away in your back pocket. Other fathers did.

every author a merciless god

A man bends down & picks up a stick. He tosses the stick in the air. He watches it rise. He watches it fall. He contemplates the stick after it's landed. One end of the stick points east; one end, west. The man begins walking west. As he walks, he rolls his shoulders, loosening a kink. The road is slow & dusty, barely a road at all, but the man appears content with his progress. How horrible of me, then, to send a large dog trotting toward him, a severed hand hanging out of its mouth.

dot-dot-dash

1 Dot

All night I follow the same path the bullet traveled. The shadows of branches can only communicate in thin, hopeless gestures. Many of the students I taught the previous term didn't believe me when I told them that dot-dot-dash in Morse code means "Oh, shit!" The classroom clock never worked right either.

2 Dot

Look up from what you're reading. The hitchhiker on the entrance ramp might be the missing child. I've held long, imaginary conversations with him. He says the spruce tree will become a cello & the piano, because not played regularly, will forget its sound.

3 Dash

In an unfamiliar street turned down by mistake, someone is being beaten. Tiny brown birds hop about the gutter like crudely shaped souls. Call if you have any questions or if there's such a thing as cancer of the heart.

prescription

A decrepit usherette in a man's
suit coat shone her light in my face.
Nobody would tell me what I did,
only that this never happened.
The mind, the doctor said above the roar,
is an unruly puppy. Why every morning
I must swallow a pill with my juice,
the road still climbing through a dark forest
that loves the world just as it is.

errata

The roots of words, finely ground
& placed in food, are said to be a love charm.
In the wild, cognates are pollinated
by ruby-throated hummingbirds
(whereas bees are indifferent to them).
There's a book like a milky liquid that everybody's reading.
The sleeping baby has about eleven pages left.

puzzle of a downfall child

We only get the newspaper still
so she can do the Word Jumble.
She works on it standing
at the kitchen counter,
a black pen in her hand,
an agonized look on her face.
"Is 'pearlized' a word?"
she'll ask me, sounding doubtful.
Some days it takes a while
to unscramble all the letters.
When she finally does,
she reads the words out loud
for me to admire.
Scorched. Anthem. Gazing.
Machinery. Dawned.
It's like a poem, I say to myself,
just before it's a poem.

panicky anarchy

The only way through is full of crimes and rivers. There are also mirrors that plead incomprehension. It's better not to remember the cat clinging to the fiddle or the word that was scribbled in yellow on the surgical site. The last time anyone looked elements of the Soviet security apparatus remained. I point as a substitute for speaking. Someone who shouldn't have got it gets an injection. The bride and groom close their eyes when they kiss. After a week, spasms.

my imaginary invalid

There's a fuzziness to your features as if someone in a great hurry had molded them. You could try starting over, pushing another landscape over the horizon. Of course, it's the same lies everywhere, just told with different words. You suck your cracked and bleeding knuckles. The ritual stretches out for days. Sometimes you wonder whether those weeds you removed weren't actually flowers.

sanctuary

1

It used to be called the Reformed Church of Lost, Crying Children. Now it's the Church of Holy Shit! The congregation is waiting on the shore for the flames to freeze so they can cross over the yellow lake of fire. Meanwhile, I'm looking for a five-letter word that isn't "ardor."

2

I would get more results, the screen says, without quote marks around "suicidal thoughts." There's a weird old man I never met living in a cabin deep in the North Woods, with only a dancing poodle, and the books I might have written, to keep him company.

insomnia makes a strange companion

You can get your picture taken with fat Elvis or experience a serial killer's brain floating in alcohol. Branches shake where the missing children have just passed. A woman waits in bed like a satin pocket and a crust of dried blood. Death is there, too, brushing away the flies from its face.

after aurora

1

Here's the empty room that lived inside him. Here's the key he used to lock it. Here's the black moon that burned in his window. Here's the leaf he heard vibrating all night. Here's the shadow he kept for company. Here's the red hair dye he fed it. Here's the fly that chased through his dreams. Here's the twisted sheets in which he woke up flailing. Here's the trigger he caressed with his finger. Here's the fragment of a planet the cops dug out of the wall.

2

So many of us stumble out of our mothers with stricken faces, all crooked lines & lumpy shadows, that I long ago lost count. In the movie version, I would go off to live among the slandered Western wolves & a fleet of fugitive whales. Everyone in the waiting area is now waiting for a different kind of ending, earbuds in, eyes blank, departure time forever imminent.

3

One guy's telling the other guy about a new porn site, Hotel. cum. I try not to listen too closely. Meanwhile, children keep busy applying for jobs they won't get, in cities they don't want to live. I've begun to think I can feel the detonations of dreams & longings, a rumbling repeated indefinitely. And those not burned up by death rays, the guy's saying, become their slaves. Summer, the weather unpredictable everywhere you go.

4

Chilly rain rattles down like a metal grate over a storefront. Fist, stick, rock, knife, gun – nothing else grows. Anyone still alive tomorrow will live amid lightning bolts & silent bells.

the persistent dust of dangerous machines

Some nights my head is an animal. Some nights I'm slanted like a handicap ramp no one but you needs to use. Some nights I grip the steering wheel while moving at a crawl through alternating bands of development & rot. Some nights I stay inside in case there's a patrol. Some nights I stop talking, suddenly conscious of the fact that canine can mean a tooth or a dog. Some nights I can't keep the contempt out of my voice. Some nights the Lord gets shanked. Some nights He gets T-boned.

all systems tend toward collapse

1

Why stop & get out on First Degree Street, unless you have, perhaps, an ambulance. No one there knows you or wonders about you. No one informs you there's a map on the wall, one with a big red arrow &, in black, the reassuring sounding words, You Are Here.

2

The automated tellers riot at 10 & 11 & again at three. Gloria, my elderly neighbor, is right to fear a loss of connectivity, a hairline fracture, another hung jury. I myself have been waiting several decades now for my work to develop a cult following. A small adjustment might fix this, but the back of the package says, Do not insert in rectum or vagina using fingers or mechanical device. The trees shake their great shaggy heads as if they disagree.

3

Try walking toward the sun-striped hills, right, left, right, left, a girl's voice calling out from somewhere, Please, please, please. The farther you go, the bleaker the sky gets. As for the hurt bicyclist lying crumpled in the road, he can't tell you what happened. He can only tell you how welcome it felt.

bodies in motion

Think of me as your missing dog, your kitchen junk drawer, & I'll think of you as the runaway truck lane, insouciant pie, why light blasts from our bedroom window, the noise so noisy the neighbors threaten to call the noise police. Don't they know there's no such thing? There's only one law, the preposterous prehistoric law of gravity. Go ahead, disorganize my hardware, commit my body to the deep, the world needs our casual desecrations, it needs us to fly.

tiny mummies

Rain falls
like the dead

crawling
from their tombs.

the part of the world i'm in

1

When night falls on my town, all the dogs bark insanely & the lights of a plane get mistaken for stars.

2

Bank fees! Speed traps! Cable blackouts! So what? There are diamonds & sapphires & barbells in eruption, & holy shit! they're everywhere. I wait up all night for just one blast to lift me.

3

It's a good thing you're not here. The fire in my head is apparently still too hot to approach. Plus, the politicians are all talking at once & I can't remember where I hid the last time that happened.

4

Siddhartha went searching for a way toward the vast, tiny snow that pats my hair in the parking lot of Mama's Donuts & More.

About the Author

Howie Good, a journalism professor at SUNY New Paltz, is the author of more than two dozen chapbooks and several full-length poetry collections. His poetry has been honored with nomination for the Pushcart Prize and the Best of Net anthology multiple times. He co-edits *White Knuckle Press* with Dale Wisely.